AROUND
CHIPPING NORTON
IN OLD PHOTOGRAPHS
A SECOND SELECTION

D1332902

AROUND
CHIPPING NORTON
IN OLD PHOTOGRAPHS
A SECOND SELECTION

COLLECTED BY
THE CHIPPING NORTON LOCAL HISTORY SOCIETY

ALAN SUTTON
1989

Alan Sutton Publishing
Gloucester

First published 1989

British Library Cataloguing in Publication Data

Around Chipping Norton in old photographs : a second selection.
1. Oxfordshire. Chipping Norton, history
I. Chipping Norton Local History Society
942.5'71

ISBN 0-86299-657-0

Typesetting and origination by
Alan Sutton Publishing
Printed in Great Britain by
Dotesios Printers Limited

CONTENTS

INTRODUCTION

Situated on the northern slopes of the Cotswolds, Chipping Norton, 650 ft above sea level, is the highest town in the county. The Cotswold-stone houses and the tree-lined approaches encourage visitors to take a longer look at the old town.

The centre of the town is on two different levels with some splendid eighteenth century houses on the High Street which, apart from the filling-in of the archway at the White Hart, the closure of the Black Boy Yard and the demolition of the Old Red Lion which formerly stood across the bottom of the Cattle Market, remains very much as it did 150 years ago.

By the Charter of Incorporation of the Borough in 1606, it was established that the town should be governed by a Corporation consisting of two Bailiffs and twelve Burgesses. Although the old Guildhall had been used as the Town Hall, this was not, as might be supposed, the usual meeting place of the worthy Corporation. Their business was transacted at the various hostelries in the town, where refreshments were an important part of the proceedings. Under the Municipal Corporations Act of 1835 the government of the town became vested in a Mayor, four Aldermen and twelve Burgesses. The new council was apparently very impressed with their dignified position and the old Guildhall was no longer thought grand enough for them. It was therefore decided to build a new Town Hall and this was erected in 1842 to the design of George Repton. Upon the site chosen for the new Town Hall there formerly stood a market hall; a flat-roofed building supported by nine stone pillars and fully exposed to the winds. A more draughty site for the transaction of business could not be imagined! Adjoining the market hall was an elm tree occupied from time immemorial by rooks as a rookery. The rooks were apparently held in great esteem by the townspeople and there was great opposition to it being felled to make way for the Town Hall. One of the stone pillars, forming part of the old market hall, can still be seen on the lower side of the Town Hall.

The name of the town, 'Chipping' from the Saxon word 'ceapen' indicating a market, reflects the importance of the town in the Middle Ages, when the district had become famous for its woollen industry. It was the Medieval wool merchants who re-built the fine Perpendicular church, with its unusual hexagonal porch, a priest's room and bell turret above. The nave of the church carries right through to the clerestory which fills the church with light. The memorial brasses have been lifted from the floor and are mounted on the walls of St John's Chapel. The merchants are depicted standing on woolsacks, the symbol of their trade, which produced the wealth that enabled them to build the church. A vicar who refused to use Cranmer's English prayer book was condemned to hang from his own steeple. The association with the woollen industry was continued when William Bliss established his factory in New Street in the eighteenth century and built up a great reputation for the manufacture of tweeds. Such was the popularity of his cloth that he was able to build a modern mill in the valley in 1855. This mill was destroyed by fire in 1872 and three workers lost their lives. It was re-erected within 12 months. The mill had a splendid reputation for its relationship with the owners and the workers, which was only marred by a bitter strike in 1913. The mill ceased production in 1980 and has now been converted into luxury living accommodation.

Chipping Norton stood on the old coaching route to Worcester, with the 'Sovereign' and the 'Blenheim' making the journey from London and staging at the White Hart. The amount of traffic passing this way had been sufficient for the Court Baron and Court Leet to make an order in 1822 'that any persons permitting any waggon, cart or other carriage to stand in any of the public streets or lanes with the borough (particularly the narrow near the Blue Boar) more than eight hours or for a longer time than is absolutely necessary for loading or unloading, shall incure a penalty of five shillings.' With the advent of the railway in 1855 the position altered and the road traffic greatly diminished. The railway survived for just over a hundred years before closing down and events have now turned full circle with traffic returning to the roads and the narrow part by the Blue Boar still proving a problem.

An event which was to prove of great importance to the town occurred in 1871 when Mr Thomas Brassey, the great railway builder, bought Heythrop mansion. It was destroyed by fire in 1840 and had stood derelict and roofless, the walks and gardens a wilderness. He re-erected the stately home in more than its former glory as a wedding present for his son Albert. A great number of servants were employed at Heythrop and the vast amount of commodities required for the house provided a considerable source of income to the local tradespeople. Mr Brassey's interest in local affairs and his generosity were to prove of great benefit. He was appointed Master of the Heythrop Hounds in 1873 and continued in that capacity for 45 years.

Industrially many things have altered during the present century. The brewing industry, which was a source of income for many, has now disappeared. Nothing now remains of the tan yard in Distons Lane which produced the leather for the glove-making industry. The gas works and the electricity station have gone. To compensate for these losses, the internationally acclaimed furniture manufacturers Parker Knoll have brought much needed light industry to the town and employ more than 400 people. The Royal Label factory making motorway signs etc., also has a small factory in the town. There is significant employment too provided by the restaurants, public houses and small businesses.

It was very fortunate for Chipping Norton that, at the beginning of the present century, two photographers, Frank Packer and Percy Simms, set up business in the town. It is largely owing to their endeavours with the many thousands of photographs they took of the buildings and events relating to the town and district, that members of The Chipping Norton Local History Society have assembled, from their collections, this second edition of *Around Chipping Norton in Old Photographs*.

Dennis Lewis
For Chipping Norton Local History Society

SECTION ONE

The Town

AN OLD PRINT showing the centre of the town with the market hall and the old elm tree, c. 1830.

MARKET PLACE in 1908.

CHILDREN around the iron fountain in 1902, which formerly stood in the Market Square.

A CARRIAGE AND HORSES in the town centre in the snow.

MAJOR DUNLOP and his family at Hill View (opposite the squash courts).

PETTIPHER'S VAN in wintertime showing Bill Guy, -?-, Mr Barnes.

DUNSTAN HOUSE, New Street, at Easter 1937.

BOTTOM SIDE, Chipping Norton.

CHIPPING NORTON MARKET in the 1960s.

ALBERT BRASSEY. In 1871 Thomas Brassey, the great railway builder, bought Heythrop mansion which, 40 years earlier, had been destroyed by fire. He re-erected the stately home as a wedding present for his son Albert. A great number of servants were employed and goods required for the house provided a considerable income for the Chipping Norton tradespeople. He became a great benefactor to the town and supported many local causes. In 1873 he was elected Master of the Heythrop Hounds and continued as Master for 45 years.

MARKET STREET, 1919.

CHIPPING NORTON MARKET SQUARE c. 1880.

THE HIGH STREET in Edwardian times.

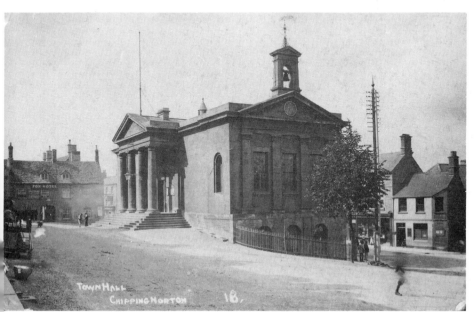

THE TOWN HALL.

CHIPPING NORTON CO-OPERATIVE SOCIETY — the butcher's shop in the High Street. Joe Goodman is on the right of the picture.

CHIPPING NORTON CO-OPERATIVE SOCIETY — the new butcher's shop in West Street. Ben Hovard, Cyril Smart, Jim Shepherd, Bill Fiddler, George Withers, George Beard, Fred Haynes and Frank Jarvis. This shop is now occupied by 'Highlights'.

MR AND MRS LANHAM outside the Victoria Restaurant – now 'Highlights' in West Street.

MR A.E. COOMBES, the local taxidermist. He later kept a barber's shop in Middle Row. He was also a member of the Volunteer Fire Brigade.

CHIPPY BULL. 'Chippy' Bull was a well-known character in Chipping Norton. He is best remembered for his remarkable feat in 1870 of pushing half a ton up New Street in a wheelbarrow for a wager. He later had a bookmaker's business in Paris. He then ran the Royal Adelaide Hotel, Windsor, where J.L. Sullivan, the World Heavy Weight Champion, made his headquarters when he came to England in 1888.

THE TARMAC GANG: Harry Powers, Mr Wallington, Mr Collett, -?-, Perce Kerry, -?-, Bill Johnson, Fred Shayler, Randy Burden, -?-, -?-.

FLOODS IN WEST STREET after a bad thunderstorm. Packer's Shoe Shop is on the left.

ROWELL & SONS – Ironworks. Left – Wilf Barnes and the Coles Brothers.

THE HUB IRONWORKS STAND at the Public Works Road & Transport Exhibition & Congress – 1931.

MR COLSTON'S GROCERY SHOP in New Street. It was demolished in 1968.

LOOKING TOWARDS BURFORD CORNER from the west.

HIGH STREET.

THE OPENING OF THE FOOTBALL SEASON. 'Waiting for the Green-un' (*The Sporting Mail*).

HIGH STREET showing the Blue Anchor public house.

HAROLD LORD outside his baker's shop in High Street in 1933.

NEW STREET before demolition in 1968.

... AND AFTERWARDS a photograph taken in 1989.

THE OXFORDSHIRE AGRICULTURAL SHOW being advertised in West Street.

WEST END, Chipping Norton in 1906.

FLIGHT SUB-LIEUT. H.R.SIMMS. R.N.A.S. OF CHIPPING NORTON, WHO BROUGHT DOWN A HOSTILE AEROPLANE WHICH FELL IN FLAMES CLOSE TO THE BELGIAN LINES THE COMBAT AND RESULT BEING IN FULL VIEW OF THE BELGIAN SOLDIERS IN THE TRENCHES. FEBY 29. 1916.

Flight Sub-Lieut. Simms was the son of D.R. Simms, jeweller of Chipping Norton. He was later killed in action and his body was returned to Chipping Norton for burial.

WEST STREET, Chipping Norton, 1906.

MEDIEVAL CELLAR in No. 20 High Street.

THE REAR of the White Hart Hotel.

THE TOMB of Thomas and Elizabeth Rickardes in St Mary's Church.

TIMMS' SHOP in Horse Fair.

THE ROYAL OAK and The Bugle, Horse Fair.

TOWNS END, Chipping Norton with: -?-, Mr Margetts and Bill Fifield.

THE LABOUR EXCHANGE, Town's End – formerly Folland's Factory.

PANORAMIC VIEW of Over Norton Road, Banbury Road, Oxford Road and Rock Hill.

CHIPPING NORTON from the air.

AERIAL PHOTOGRAPH of Chipping Norton showing the top of New Street, as it was before demolition.

ROCK HILL.

LOOKING DOWN Rock Hill, c. 1907.

CHIPPING NORTON WORKHOUSE c. 1920.

Mr John Shadbolt driving Burden's cart in Albion Street.

DISTONS LANE. The houses on the left were built by Wm. Bliss in 1879 for his workers.

THE GREAT BLIZZARD, Distons Lane, showing the Old Tannery on the left in 1916.

DENNIS AND EILEEN LEWIS, all dressed up in the playground at the New Street Infants School waiting to receive their peace mugs in 1918. Shortly after leaving school Dennis took a great interest in the history of Chipping Norton and over the past 60 years he has acquired a vast number of documents etc., relating to the town. He has recently written a book called *Chipping Norton Inns*.

SPRING STREET (Tite End).

THE CASTLE BANKS, Chipping Norton.

COT LANE, Chipping Norton.

MR MARGETTS bringing the milk home with a yoke through the Cleeves.

A VIEW OF OVER NORTON ROAD before urbanization.

A MODERN PHOTOGRAPH of Over Norton Road.

CHAPEL HOUSE COTTAGE.

THE ORIGINAL QUIET WOMAN PUBLIC HOUSE, Southcombe.

THE DEMOLITION of the chimney of Hitchman's Brewery in Albion Street.

THE DEMOLITION OF GUILDHALL PLACE by Mr Eddy Bennett.

MR & MRS HEPBURN selling Sunday newspapers by the Guildhall 1936.

THE OPENING OF THE SPAR SHOP in High Street: Mrs R. Drinkwater, Mrs Clandfield, Mrs Joan Dix, Mrs Wilson, Mrs Chittendon, Mrs Church.

THE INTERIOR of the Regent Cinema in New Street.

THE REGENT CAFE, New Street.

Transport
and Bliss Mills

MRS GRACE PACKER with Chipping Norton station in the background.

A VIEW through the road bridge to the tunnel.

THE GENERAL STRIKE of 1926. Those shown are: E. Johnston, Mr Morse, Mr Rowell.

A GWR AEC DIESEL CAR in the station.

'WALLACE', the station cat.

THE CO-OPERATIVE COAL WHARF at the railway yard. Those shown include: Latham, Jesse Hadland, Tom Hill, Alf Doman, Charlie Winnett (foreman), Jack Bolter.

THE OXFORD UNIVERSITY OFFICER TRAINING CORPS loading guns at Chipping Norton station.

THE 'HEYTHROP GIANTS' being taken to Chipping Norton station by C.R. Claridge and Sons in 1926. At 75 ft long, the larch trees, to be used as ships' masts, became wedged at New Street corner, lifting the horses off the ground. They were only freed after 20 ft had been cut off the end of the trees. The RSPCA took Claridges to court for cruelty but the horsemen explained that the horses only responded to kindness and had a token fine of £1.

C. R. CLARIDGE & SONS transporting timber from Heythrop to the station on their way to their sawmills at Exeter.

HITCHMANS WAGONS outside their offices in West Street.

MR BARNES with Pettipher's van in 1931.

A POLICEMAN and George Hughes inspecting the damage after a road crash.

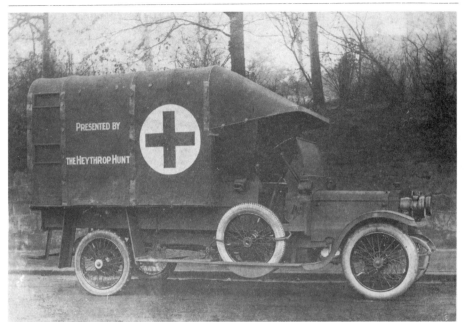

THE AMBULANCE presented by the Heythrop Hunt for the use of the Army, 1915.

A LOAD OF HAY overturned at the top of New Street.

THE BANBURY BUS.

THE OXFORD BUS GARAGE in Albion Street in 1947. Seen here are: Joe Arnold, Jim Robinson, ? Green, Ron Abbott, -?-, Alf Bridges.

AN EARLY PHOTOGRAPH of the Lower Bliss Mill, built in 1855 and destroyed by fire in 1872, showing the workmen's cottages at the rear.

THESE TWO PHOTOGRAPHS show the remains of the Lower Bliss Mill after the fire which was started by a boiler exploding at 5.45 am on 7 February 1872. Three men, Thomas Cook, Thomas Peachy and Richard Boscott were killed by the fire. The mill, which was totally destroyed, had only been built in 1855, but a new mill was built and manufacturing tweed within a year. None of the workers lost their jobs as the company used the old upper mill as the rebuilding was being done.

THE LOWER MILL, Chipping Norton.

THE HOUSE built by William Bliss the Second in New Street – later occupied by Mr Dunstan who managed the Bliss Mill. It has now been demolished to make way for Dunstan Avenue.

THE SITTING ROOM of Bliss' House in New Street.

THE POLICE in Chipping Norton for the strike at Bliss Mill in 1913.

THE MILL STRIKE. A scene outside the police court after the trial of one of the strikers.

Events
and Occasions

MANCHESTER HOUSE and the adjoining shop decorated for the Coronation of Edward VII, 1902.

A PROCESSION through the town to celebrate the Coronation of Edward VII, 1902.

CELEBRATION of the Coronation of George V in 1911.

CORONATION CELEBRATIONS for George V in New Street. Mrs Carey and son Herbert outside their shop.

CORONATION CELEBRATIONS 1911. Mr Herbert and staff outside his shop in New Street.

TOWN COUNCIL ELECTION in 1909.

THE GENERAL ELECTION in 1910. Robert Brassey and his family canvassing.

PLANTING THE CORONATION TREE, 1911, with George Mace and Charlie Simms.

TREE PLANTING in Hailey Road by Mr Freeman to celebrate the coronation in 1937. Also present: Frank Morris, Town Clerk; W.J. Whettam, Borough Surveyor; Robert Major, D.R. Rutter, J. Marshall, B. Harris, A.A. Webb, George Warmington and Walter Craft.

REAT FLYING EVENT AT CHIPPING NORTON — 27. THE AEROPLANE ARRIVES ON THE FIELD

REAT FLYING EVENT AT CHIPPING NORTON — FITTING UP THE AEROPLANE

Great Flying Event at Chipping Norton. 10. Mr Gustav Hamel's Aeroplane

Mr Gustav Hamel ready to fly —   Packer Photo

GUSTAV HAMEL giving a flying display at Chipping Norton on 27 February 1913. He came to the town with his aeroplane by train and was transported to the Brewery Field by horse and cart where the plane was assembled and the display given. Gustav Hamel was one of the pioneer pilots. He had carried the first official air mail from Hendon to Windsor in 1911. In 1913 he won the Round London Air Race with a speed of 75 mph. In 1914 he looped the loop fourteen times in 17 minutes in the presence of King George V and Queen Mary of Windsor. Later that year he was lost in the Channel when flying a new machine from Paris to England.

MR H.Y. ALLEN, a Band of Hope member.

THE BAND OF HOPE PROCESSION. Mr Fred Lewis is holding the reins.

THE BAPTIST UNION CARAVAN MISSION outside the Guildhall. Bill Hunt and Fred Burbidge standing on the van.

CHIPPING NORTON TEMPERANCE SOCIETY. Mrs T. Burden, Mrs P. Burden, Miss Naimby, Mrs Arnett, Mrs Mason, Mrs Bound. Sitting: Mrs Simpson, Mrs Bond, Mrs Franklin, Mrs P. Simms, Mrs Street.

THE OPENING of the Children's Hospital and Convalescent Home, Thursday 2 June 1904.

CHILDREN HAVING TREATMENT at the National Children's Home and Orphanage in New Street.

THE ENTRANCE to the National Children's Home in Chipping Norton.

CHIPPING NORTON METHODIST BAND.

A PARTY for the residents of the workhouse.

224LBS OF POTATOES grown from 1lb of seed by Henry Tidmarsh – shown here with his two sons Henry and Dennis.

OXFORDSHIRE RIFLE VOLUNTEERS at camp at Aldershot in 1892. Jim Bunting, -?-, Bill Gibbs, Tommy Pratt, Hubert Cook and Jimmy Robinson.

A PHOTOGRAPH taken on the wedding day of King George V and Queen Mary, 6 July 1893 shows the Oxon & Bucks Volunteers Band: ? Grantham, Tom Pratt, Chas Heath, Geo Compton, Sid Little, Fred Baker, Geo Miles, Fred Tilling, Harry Absolam, Alf King. Bottom row: Aubrey Porter, Fred Meads, Harry Tilling, Webster Cox, A. Cox, Mr Hannis, Frank Burden.

ST JOHN'S AMBULANCE BRIGADE setting off for the Royal Review at Windsor, 22 June 1912.

ST JOHN'S AMBULANCE BRIGADE leaving for military service from the station in August 1914.

THE NATIONAL RESERVES leaving for Southampton on 25 November 1914.

OFFICERS of the 52nd Regiment (Oxford & Bucks) Light Infantry in Chipping Norton on 21 September 1913. The photograph was taken at the rear of the Crown Hotel with Mr James, the proprietor, on the left.

CHIPPING NORTON SPECIAL POLICE in 1914. Top row: Mr Candy, Bert Buggins, Jim Smart, Frank Lewis.

THE GPO erecting one of their poles outside the Blue Boar.

THE CHRISTENING of the new fire engine 'King George' by the Mayor, W.C. Hannis in 1932.

HOSPITAL SATURDAY, 1916. The ride provided by the Boy Scouts.

AN OX ROAST in Chipping Norton.

FRED LEWIS with his 'Bathing Belles' at Chipping Norton Hospital Saturday in 1920.

HOSPITAL SATURDAY – D.R. Simms is on the right.

CHIPPING NORTON HOSPITAL SATURDAY. Mr W. Johnston with Reg Johnston driving the horses.

CHIPPING NORTON HOSPITAL SATURDAY 1929 depicting Misery Farm. The houses to the rear formerly stood at the bottom of the green. Reg Johnston and Arthur Sale on the farm!

CHIPPING NORTON HOSPITAL SATURDAY 1989 — 13

HOSPITAL SATURDAY, 1939. Ted Simms driving his float in Albion Street.

MR REGINALD JOHNSTON, one of Chipping Norton's well-known characters. Reg Johnston worked with his father in the saddlery and shoe repairing business in West Street. His country accent secured him a part in *The Archers* serial on the BBC. He supported many good causes, particularly the National Children's Homes and his amusing floats on Hospital Saturdays were one of the highlights of the procession.

MR REG JOHNSTON and friend on stilts in the High Street.

HOSPITAL SATURDAY 1938. The Keep Fit class with their float.

BLISS TWEED and Chipping Norton Carnival, 1939.

MAYPOLE DANCING in Chipping Norton town centre.

THE TUG OF WAR at Chipping Norton Church Fête in 1928. The Council School winning team included: Frank Shepard, Charlie Morse, Roy Woodward, Fred Anson (teacher), Wally Pickett, Balfour, Norman Cox, Balfour, Norman Keen, Dennis Lewis, Dennis Brain, Bob Turner, -?-, Bob Sewell, Cecil Watts, -?-, Frank Perry, Dick Turner, -?-, Hepburn, -?-.

FRED BURBIDGE collecting a swarm of bees in Horse Fair.

STOUR CHORAL UNION 22nd Festival Division B, 1930. Back row: -?-, W. Pettipher, Mr Whettam. Second row: W. Burson, -?-, -?-, -?-, E. Moulder, Miss Jackson, -?-, N. Bolter, Mr Moulder, -?-. First row: -?-, -?-, -?-, -?-, Mr Kemp, Miss Ann Hawkyard, -?-, Mrs F. Burbidge, Mrs Pettipher. Front row: -?-, -?-, Rene Medley.

THE ROUNDABOUT at 'the Mop'.

THE DEDICATION AND PRESENTATION of the British Legion standard July 1929. The Mayor, Mr Gardiner, Ike Castle, Revd Arkle. On the extreme right; Major Young.

PUSH-BALL at the British Legion Fête in 1929. S. Nason, H. Harris, C. Robinson, -?-, Darky Hawtin, Mr Haney, -?- and Ike Castle were present.

SILVER JUBILEE PARTY in Finsbury Place, 1935.

FLOODS after a cloudburst in Horse Fair in 1938.

FLOODING AT THE GASWORKS after the thaw in 1947. George Heritage and Len Bench.

THE ARRIVAL OF THE EVACUEES at Chipping Norton station on 1 September 1939.

THE FIRST AIR RAID WARNING on 6 September 1939 in Chipping Norton.

SPRING STREET VJ-Day tea party in 1945.

GEORGE ARLISS, the well-known film star, on his way to The Mount.

THE MOUNT. The Mount was built by Henry Field Wilkins in 1869. It was constructed on the site of what was formerly the baillie or keep of the castle which formerly stood near the church. Alderman Wilkins, a solicitor was a direct descendant of Oliver Cromwell and was a much respected resident of the town. He was the only Jubilee Mayor in the kingdom who had been mayor in 1837 and 1887. George Arliss, the film star, whose best known film was *Disraeli*, was a frequent visitor to The Mount when he came to England from America.

THE OPENING OF THE CHILDREN'S PLAYGROUND in New Street, 30 March 1939.

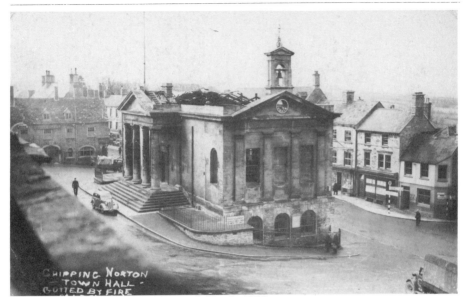

THE TOWN HALL after the great fire on 9 March 1950.

H.A. BENNETTS EMPLOYEES outside the bungalows in Walterbush Road.

A WEDDING at St Mary's Church – Robert Haynes is riding postillion.

CHIPPING NORTON POLICE escorting the bride and groom!

THE WEDDING of Mr Norman Burbidge and Miss Sylvia Craft.

WEDDING OF BANDMASTER W. H. PICKETT
AND MISS E.M. KITCHEN
— AUG. 15. 1938 —

THE WEDDING of bandmaster Mr Pickett.

THE INSTALLATION of the first Lady Mayor, Miss S. Webb, in Chipping Norton, 2 May 1950.

FLAMING JUNE. The Festival Show in 1951 opened by Mr A. Dodds-Parker MP.

SIR MICHAEL REDGRAVE opening the Art Exhibition at the Coronation celebrations in 1953.

THE MAYOR, Miss S. Webb, at Chipping Norton Festival of Britain celebrations in 1951.

CHIPPING NORTON FIRE BRIGADE at the Festival of Britain celebrations 1951. W. Reason, George Morris, Harry White, Norman Scarsbrook, Bill Wright, E. Hickman, Arthur Wearing, Bob Naylor and George Heritage were present.

TELEPHONISTS at the manual exchange, Chipping Norton Post Office.

CHIPPERFIELD'S ELEPHANTS going through the town on their way to their winter quarters in Heythrop.

THE SILVER BAND FÊTE in 1953. The bandmaster Mr Pickett seen here with the Latcham twins.

THE SILVER BAND FÊTE in 1955. When is the public house to be built in Walterbush Road? (It wasn't!) Jim Watkins, Albert Allen, Sid Hitchcox, Boxer Griffin, Dick Hicks.

PRIZE WINNERS at the Horticultural Association Annual Show: E. Brown, Reg Beale, -?-, -?-, Mrs Brindle, Arthur Brindle, Mr Edginton, -?-, Leonard Miles, Major Gen. Sir Montague Stopford, Lady Stopford, The Hon. Peter Ward, Mrs P. Ward, Rachel Ward and Mr A. Swann.

HARVEST FESTIVAL at the Red Lion, Chipping Norton.

THE LADIES FROM BLISS MILL playing football for a charity match in the 1950s.

CHIPPING NORTON swimming pool.

Sport and Organizations

A GATHERING OF POACHERS with a gamekeeper outside the Brewers Arms in Albion Street.

THE MEET AT BOLTERS BARN 2

A MEET of the Heythrop Hunt at Boulter's Barn in 1915.

EXERCISING THE HOUNDS in the snow.

THE MEET AT CHIPPING NORTON showing Mr Frank Packer taking a photograph. The photographer on the steps is unknown and the photograph itself was taken by Percy Simms.

CHIPPING NORTON Blue Boys Baseball Team in 1936. Charlie Robinson, John Shadbolt, Stan Franklin, Ray Gardener, -?-, Jack Harding, Mr Withers, Dennis Lowe, Charlie Withers, John Beck. Front row: Bill Thornton, Kit Harding, Roy Burford, -?-, Cecil Giles.

WHEN FRED LEWIS, one of Chipping Norton's best-loved and colourful characters, formed one of the earliest troops of Boy Scouts in Britain in 1907, he looked for a game which could be played by a group of boys. He therefore introduced baseball in 1910 and founded the Chipping Norton Baseball Club in 1920. By his great interest in the game he earned for himself the sobriquet 'the Father of British Baseball'. He took the business founded by his father in 1928 and carried on as Funeral Undertaker, Heating Engineer, Builder, etc., until 1957. A great sportsman, in his younger days he played football, tennis, golf, cycling and was a useful runner. He ran shows with his magic lantern and on the occasion of a great fire in the High Street in 1900 showed slides of the event at his magic lantern show the same night. He was also very active in organizing Hospital Saturdays which raised many thousands of pounds. He died in 1960 aged 79.

FRED LEWIS with the Baseball Club on a Sunday afternoon at Banbury Road diamond c. 1953.

CHIPPING NORTON CYCLE CLUB at Great Tew in 1898.

CHIPPING NORTON GOLF CLUB in 1924. Back row: W. Hamblett, -?-, Mr Brookbanks, -?-, J.C. Rowell, -?-. Second row: -?-, -?-, -?-, A.A. Webb, -?-, -?-, -?-, Mrs Hamblett, -?-, -?-, -?-, -?-, -?-. Third row: Mr Hamblett Snr, -?-, Frank Morris, Mrs Webb, -?-, Mr Cooper, Fred Lewis.

NED SUMPTER AND COD ROBINSON: two local 'grasstrack' racers.

BILLIARDS TEAM at the Liberal Club including: Hubert Packer, Alf Carter, -?-, Les Chapman, Mr Townsend, Aubrey Aldridge, Edgar Johnston.

CHIPPING NORTON FOOTBALL CLUB 1948–9: winners of Oxon Charity Cup. The team included: Austin Smith, Mr Rose, Norman Lyne, P. Baucham, Wally Timms, Sid Moulder, Derek Jarvis, C. Withers, Harry White, Billy Aldridge, Tony Padley, John Beck, Frank Miles and E. Widdows.

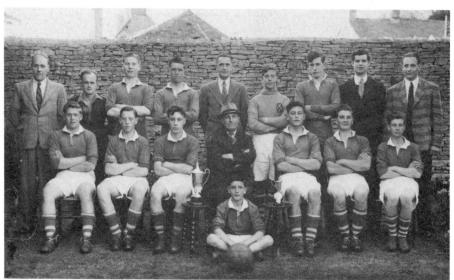

CHIPPING NORTON MINORS 1950–1: Reg Benfield, Ray Simms, Mr Hovard, -?-, G. Tompkins, Fred Panting, Peter Grant, Doug Reeves, J.W. Roberts, Philip Nicks, Mr Heritage, ? Smith, -?-, Brian Heritage and David Hovard.

BOWYER LODGE OF FREEMASONS. -?-, -?-, -?-, O. Carrington, -?-, -?-, -?-, -?-, -?-, Arthur Brindle, Edgar Smith, Mr Swann, -?-, Col. Schofield, -?-, -?-, Dr Russell, F.W.P. Matthews, W.N. Rowell.

ATC 136 SQUADRON at the main entrance to the grammar school.

THE ARMY CADETS. The new unit was founded at Chipping Norton on 13 January 1959. Those included are: Mayor S.D. Wykes, Gen. Sir Montague Stopford, Col. H.D. Goldie, Major E. Inge, Revd C.A. Crofts (chaplain), Capt. Peter Robinson, Ted Jones, Bill Kennedy, Geoff Robinson.

MR PERRY'S PEACE BAND.

THE GIRLS BRITISH SCHOOL 1920. Top row: -?- Homes, Queenie Brown, Gwen Bates, -?- Tucker, Rennie Medley, Phylis Brooks, -?- Homes. Second row: -?- Homes, -?- Barnes, Elsie Pratt, -?-, -?-, Molly Hess, Cath Sharman. Third row: -?- Homes, -?- Homes, Etty Butler, -?- Bench, Kath Hieath, -?- Parsons, -?-, -?-, -?- Sewell, Eileen Lewis, Edna Winnett, Lona Bench. Bottom row: Ruth Harris (on chair), Etta Wearing, -?- Woodward, Cath Hewitt, Dill Smith, -?- Bench, -?- Drury, -?- Drury, Doll Pinfold, -?- (kneeling) and Frances Keen.

CHIPPING NORTON CHURCH SCHOOL COOKERY CLASS taking a breath of fresh air outside the Oddfellows Hall.

CHIPPING NORTON Church of England Girls' School in 1938.

CHIPPING NORTON SCHOOL OF DANCING — Miss Trump with the ballet dancers.

CHIPPING NORTON BOY SCOUTS.

CHIPPING NORTON SCOUT GROUP in the late 1940s. The scoutmaster was Mr Ron Stares and his assistant was Mr Ernest Sandles.

THE GUIDES off to camp with their leaders, Miss Sylvia Rose and Mrs Olive Williams. Also shown are: Clare Hargreaves, Joanna Leonard, Hilary Pulker, Sarah Morris, Sarah Howes, Heidi Housden, Diana Morris, Alison King, Susan King, Julie Howes, Caroline Harper, Sarah Fox and Heather Tyler.

THE PDSA VAN in Chipping Norton including: A. Brindle, Beryl Johnston, A. Pick, Jean Helmore, Jackie Townley, Margot Rivers, Peter Bridges, Paul Ashmore, Pat Carter, Don Branson, Robin Woodcock and D. Johnson.

BELLRINGERS at Chipping Norton: -?-, Sid Pulker, Reg Jarvis, Harry Francis, W. Hutchinson and Mary Pulker.

SONGS OF PRAISE in Chipping Norton Church.

SENIOR MEMBERS of the Keep Fit Club. Shown are: -?-, Joan Burden, Valerie Bennett, Pat Harding, Joy Newman, Mabel Perry, -?-, Dorothy Burden, Eileen Bolter, Jackie Townley, Marion Hoare, Nina Haney, Wendy Burford, Pat Fletcher.

THE JUNIOR KEEP FIT CLUB: Mrs J. Newman and Mrs M. Perry, Pat Bennett, G. Ackerman, Janet Keen, Coral Morshall, -?-, Ann McDowell, Anna Watkins, Jean Coltman, Susan Johns, Wendy Simmonds, Jenny Stickley, Denise Perry, Catherine Clacy, Elspeth McDowell, Sonia Simmonds, Ann Peachey, -?-, Daphne Williams, Susan Kitchen.

Villages

OVER NORTON HILL in Edwardian times.

OVER NORTON HOUSE.

THE FELLING OF THE OLD ELM TREE at Over Norton, Easter Monday 1914.

OVER NORTON. The planting of the Coronation Tree in 1937.

MAY DAY CELEBRATIONS at Over Norton in 1938.

THE UNICORN INN at Great Rollright.

THE BUILDING OF THE HOOK NORTON VIADUCT 1883–87. Three men lost their lives during the building.

THE RAILWAY HOTEL, Hook Norton. It is now closed.

SCOTLAND END, Hook Norton.

WINNER of the 'Gordon Bennett' race at Hook Norton.

NABOTH'S VINEYARD and the Litchfield Arms at Enstone.

LOOKING DOWN THE HILL at Neat Enstone in 1904.

CHURCH ENSTONE.

THE SKELETON OF A WHALE in the grotto at Heythrop Park.

CORONATION DINNER in 1937 at Heythrop.

A CO-OP VAN at Heythrop village.

THE CHURCHILL ARMS at Ascott-under-Wychwood.

FÊTE at Ascott-Under-Wychwood in 1913.

A VIEW OF CHARLBURY from Sandford Mount.

CHARLBURY,

One Mile from the Plain where

FOREST FAI

Has usually been held, but which is now discontinued.

The Inhabitants of Charlbury respectfully inform
Public, that they intend holding a FAIR at Charlb
on *Wednesday* and *Thursday* the 14th and 15t
September, in consequence of Wychwood Forest I
being discontinued; assuring those who honour Ch
bury with their company, that every accommoda
and amusement will be afforded, on reasonable te

Booths will be erected in the Playing Close.

September 3, 1831.   [SMITH, PRINTER, C. NORT

POSTER for Charlbury Forest Fair in September 1831.

144

OLD CHARLBURY.

ST MARY'S CHURCH, Charlbury.

BROOK END, Chadlington, 1904.

LANGSTON HOUSE, Chadlington, built by James Langston of Sarsden for the curate.

IDBURY.

A GARDEN FÊTE at Bruern Abbey in 1914. Horseman-Bailey family on the left.

THE ELMS, Milton-under-Wychwood: now the offices of local builders A. Groves & Sons.

HIGH STREET, Milton-under-Wychwood.

PRINCESS MARGARET attending a church service at Milton-under-Wychwood while staying at Bruern Abbey.

RED HORSE INN, Shipton-under-Wychwood, at the turn of the century.

THE STATION ROAD TILL WORKS at Shipton-Under-Wychwood. Ernie Souch is in the foreground and George Slatter is on the left.

A HENRY TAUNT VIEW of Church Street, Shipton-under-Wychwood.

LYNEHAM SCHOOL in Edwardian times.

CORONATION CELEBRATIONS at Lyneham, 1937.

CORNWELL VILLAGE.

THE COUNTRY'S SMALLEST CO-OPERATIVE STORE at Cornwell, Mr and Mrs Deeley on the left, Lord and Lady Crichton-Stuart with the man on the right unknown.

THE PLOUGH INN and old school at Salford.

SALFORD CLUB in 1909.

A ROAD ACCIDENT outside the Cross Hands Inn.

CHASTLETON VILLAGE.

A FÊTE at Chastleton in 1936.

BENTLEY BURROWS planting a tree for the 1953 Coronation at Kingham.

COTTAGES on the Green at Kingham.

DUCK END, Kingham, with Mr Percy Simms' motor bike in the foreground.

THE FOUNTAIN at Churchill in the 1880s.

ACKNOWLEDGEMENTS

Edited and compiled by Alan Watkins • Introduction by Dennis Lewis • Typed by Brenda Morris • Photographs kindly lent by Alan Brain • Madge Byford • Keith Cooper-Harris • Eileen Forbes • Ted Jones • Dennis Lewis • Brenda Morris • Pete Scarsbrook • Alan Watkins • and from the Chipping Norton Local History Society's own collection.